MONTANA'S LAST HANGING

MONTANA'S LAST HANGING

GRACE LARSON

Montana's Last Hanging

Copyright © 2021 by Grace Larson. All rights reserved.

No part of this publication may be reproduced, stored in a retrieval system or transmitted in any way by any means, electronic, mechanical, photocopy, recording or otherwise without the prior permission of the author except as provided by USA copyright law.

The opinions expressed by the author are not necessarily those of URLink Print and Media.

1603 Capitol Ave., Suite 310 Cheyenne, Wyoming USA 82001
1-888-980-6523 | admin@urlinkpublishing.com

URLink Print and Media is committed to excellence in the publishing industry.

Book design copyright © 2021 by URLink Print and Media. All rights reserved.

Published in the United States of America
Library of Congress Control Number: 2021908981
ISBN 978-1-64753-799-9 (Paperback)
ISBN 978-1-64753-800-2 (Hardback)
ISBN 978-1-64753-801-9 (Digital)

19.04.21

Grace's mother and stepfather were all dressed up and ready to observe the hanging of Phillip "Slim" Coleman, a black man in Missoula, Montana. Her parents were among the few who had been invited to watch this man die. Grace was almost 3 years old. Coleman died September 10, 1943, and Grace would be 3 November 22 of that year. Grace's parents must have discussed the horrible crime and the gruesome hanging where Grace could hear. Their descriptions had to be traumatic for Grace to remember this.

This last legal execution in the State of Montana was overseen by Sheriff MacLean. Philip "Slim" Coleman Jr., 24 years old, was accused of viciously killing Carl and Roslyn Pearson at Lothrop, Montana. Lothrop began in the 1890's as a railroad station near the confluence of Petty Creek and the Clark Fork River. It was named for L.R. Lothrop, a Northern Pacific construction engineer.

The following is taken from Executed today.com

Coleman had robbed Carl and Roslyn Pearson of $200. He escaped in the Pearson's car, which was found in Drummond. A large manhunt was activated by Sheriff MacLean. From the time Coleman was apprehended, he had a need to brag about his dirty deeds. He showed no remorse; instead, he was extremely cheerful and commented how 'funny' the whole situation was. He became more serious the day before his scheduled hanging. At that time, Coleman told of 23 other murders he had committed since he was 14 years old growing up in the black ghettos of St. Louis, Illinois. However, in a dictated confession the night before he died, he only gave details of eight of those murders. It is believed that none of Coleman's confessions were ever used to solve unsolved murder mysteries. Coleman had refused to be visited by the only local negro minister, Father Webster Williams. In the end, Coleman was baptized into the Catholic faith and was accompanied to the gallows by Father Henry L. Sweeney.

The gallows were specially built inside the jailhouse and the hanging was done in a very quiet dignified manner with no reporters and only a few invited guests.

Coleman started his Montana crime spree when he battered to death eighty-year-old Andrew J. Walton on July 3. The octogenarian was still alive when his sister found him the next morning, but he died in the hospital the next day without ever regaining consciousness. With no witnesses or leads, the case quickly went cold.

On July 24, Coleman and another man, Lewis Brown, were hired to work on the Northern Pacific Railroad thirty miles from Missoula. They had arrived at the train stop separately. It's unclear whether they knew each other before but on the same day, they were chummy enough to start plotting to rob and kill their boss, Carl W. Pearson.

Late that night, Coleman went to Pearson's home, woke him up, and said that Brown was ill and he had to come. Pearson grabbed a bottle of aspirin and headed out. Brown, waiting in the yard, struck him on the head, and left his body in the yard. Coleman went back inside, found Pearson's wife, Roslyn, and stabbed her to death in her bed. The men spared the couple's child, seven-year-old Richard; it was he who found the bodies the next day.

The murderers collected their loot, divided it between them and went their separate ways. Brown and Coleman were almost immediately identified as the prime suspects in the murder, and were picked up: Brown the day after the killings, and Coleman the day after Brown. Coleman was charged with Roslyn's murder, and Brown was charged with Carl's death. Both were convicted: Brown a life sentence and Coleman the death penalty.

Montana's last hanging in Missoula in 1943 was also the state's last execution for 52 years. Montana didn't execute another inmate until 1995, when Duncan McKenzie was executed by lethal injection after spending 20 years on death row. Today, lethal injection is the only death method allowed in Montana.

When I researched the Coleman hanging, only because I remembered my parents attending, I became curious and wanted more history on Montana's death penalty method of hanging.

Interesting facts on Helena, Montana Hangings from the *Independent Record*:

Helena's hangman's tree, a pillar of territorial justice, sat on the outskirts of Helena just east of Dry Gulch. There, below the mining camp's version of "boot hill," at least 10 men were lynched between 1865 and 1870, the last taking place when the vigilantes hanged Arthur Compton and Joseph Wilson for highway robbery and attempted murder.

While the crimes ranged from killing to simple theft (as was the case with the lynching of Tommy Cook in September of 1865), their fate was the same — a long rope, the slap of a horse and the inevitable tug of gravity. Tommy Cook was hanged for thieving, a sign pinned to his back stating he was a pickpocket. In October, Con Kirby swung from the tree without a note stating his crime. John- John Keene stood upon the dry goods box at the back of a wagon. A rope embraced his neck while his hands and feet were bound. The only thing that stood between him and death was the stillness of the horse. But the mob of vigilantes slapped the horse and the wagon lurched forward. On that cool June day in 1865, Keene, a wayward desperado, became the first Helena man "lynched into eternity" by the hometown boys who left his body hanging for days. In November, the vigilantes hanged George Sanders for robbing a man of $1,180 "and for other small stealings." Ah Chow was soon hanged for murder, and John "Frenchy" Crouchet was lynched for robbery. Within five years, more than 10 men, possibly 13, would hang from the tree.

In 1870, Arthur Compton and Joseph Wilson were awaiting trial for the evening robbery and the attempted murder of George Leonard. Compton and Wilson were doomed; their fates sealed. The mob hauled them across town to the dreaded Dry Gulch. They parked the wagon beneath the hangman's tree and stood the two men upon a dry goods box set at the rear of the wagon.

From Frederick Allen's book, "A Decent Orderly Lynching"

The deadliest campaign of vigilante justice in American history erupted in the Rocky Mountains during the Civil War when a private army hanged twenty-one troublemakers. Hailed as great heroes at the time, the Montana vigilantes are still revered as founding fathers.

Combing through original sources, including eye-witness accounts never before published, Frederick Allen concludes that the vigilantes were justified in their early actions, as they fought violent crime in a remote corner beyond the reach of government.

But Allen has uncovered evidence that the vigilantes refused to disband after territorial courts were in place. Remaining active for six years, they lynched more than fifty men without trials. Reliance on mob rule in Montana became so ingrained that in 1883, a Helena newspaper editor advocated a return to "decent, orderly lynching" as a legitimate tool of social control.

The following Information is from http://deathpenaltyusa.org/usa/state/montana.htm :

1.   HORAN, PETER WHITE MALE MINER MURDER HANGING AUG 25 1863 BEAVERHEAD COUNTY.

Peter Horan, a miner was hanged for murder on August 25, 1863, becoming Montana's first execution.

The crime occurred in Beaverhead County. He had murdered his mining partner, Lawrence Keeley.

2.   WHEATLEY, WILLIAM AGE 27 WHITE MALE FARM LABORER MURDER-ROBBERY HANGING AUG 13 1875 LEWIS AND CLARK COUNTY.

Wheatley and Stears had murdered Austrian immigrant Franz Warl. Mr. Warl had been tied and a rope wrapped around his neck. His skull was also crushed.

3. STEARS, WILLIAM AGE 38 BLACK MALE BARBER MURDER-ROBBERY HANGING JAN 28 1875 LEWIS AND CLARK County.

4. ROBERTS, FRANK AGE 17 WHITE MALE MURDER HANGING JAN 31, 1878 MADISON COUNTY.

Roberts was the first legal hanging in Madison County. Roberts was a Prospector who had murdered his partner.

5. KOBLE, JOSEPH WHITE MALE SOLDIER MURDER HANGING JAN 6, 1879 CHOTEAU COUNTY.

Koble and Marsh were found guilty of attempted desertion and the murder of fellow soldier, Paddy Farrell.

6. MARSH, ORLANDO, WHITE MALE SOLDIER MURDER HANGING JAN 6 1879 CHOTEAU COUNTY.

7. PELKY, PETER AGE 24 WHITE MALE RANCH HAND MURDER-ROBBERY HANGING FEB 4 1881 LEWIS AND CLARK COUNTY.

Convicted of the murder of rancher Charles Tacke.

8. DOUGLASS, JOHN AGE 37 WHITE MALE RANCH HAND MURDER HANGING MAY 27 1881 MADISON COUNTY.

Douglass was convicted of killing a Mrs. Earp who had refused his proposals many times. He shot her in the back as she was fleeing East by Stagecoach.

9. FOHRMAN, HENRY AGE 69 WHITE MALE MURDER HANGING MAY 2 1883 LEWIS AND CLARK COUNTY.

Fohrman was hanged for the murder of a fellow ranch hand.

10. AH, YOUNG ASIAN MALE LABORER MURDER-ROBBERY HANGING AUG 16 1883 MISSOULA COUNTY.

NOTE: The Chinese were considered Heathens, "Celestials," "Chinks," "Chinamen," "Orientals" and "Mongolians at this time in Montana, Ah Young was the first legal execution in Western Montana. His crime was attempting to blow up the China Paymaster's tent. He shot and killed the Chinaman who owned the tent.

Bozeman hangings that were illegal:

In 1873, John St. Clair, "Steamboat Bill," was alleged to have been a pimp who killed two young Chinese women. He and Z.A. Triplett, who had killed a man in a drunken fight, were pulled from Bozeman's log jail by a mob. Both were hanged from a slaughterhouse meat rack.

11.   CLARK, JOHN AGE 31 WHITE MALE MINER MURDER-ROBBERY HANGING DEC 27 1883 GALLATIN COUNTY,

Was hanged for the murders of Thomas Rogers and Peter Lyman.

12.   HARDING, THOMAS AGE 30 WHITE MALE MURDER-ROBBERY HANGING MAR 25 1887 BEAVERHEAD COUNTY.

Harding received the death penalty for the murder of a stagecoach driver during an attempted robbery. The execution was the first legal **hanging** in Beaverhead County.

13. HARTT, PATRICK AGE 24 WHITE MALE MURDER HANGING FEB 10 1888 LEWIS AND CLARK COUNTY.

Patrick Hartt was hanged for the murder of John W. Pitts. Hartt shot Pitts on November 7, 1885 in the court house at Boulder. Pitts was shot in the left breast and lingered to life for almost a month. It took 3 trials and an appeal to the Montana Supreme Court before Hartt was hung. His hanging was with the Jerk Type Method.

14. SCOTT, MARTIN AGE 40 WHITE MALE WOOD CHOPPER MURDER HANGING FEB 17 1888 POWELL COUNTY.

Martin Scott's wife was unfaithful and she was also a thief. She was also an alcoholic and abusive. Martin Scott had been arrested for wife abuse and paid a $25 fine. Martin Scott was found guilty of beating her to death with his gun stock and a wood chopper's sledge. He was hanged with the Jerk Hanging Method.

15. BRYSON, GEORGE WHITE MALE LABORER MURDER HANGING AUG 9 1889 JEFFERSON COUNTY.

Bryson murdered his mistress by bashing her head in. He was hanged in a jerk type gallows.

16. ROBERTS, HARRY WHITE MALE WAGON BOSS MURDER HANGING AUG 23 1889 SILVER BOW COUNTY.

Roberts shot a man that had previously attacked him in cold blood. He was hanged by the Jerk Method.

17. KING, THOMAS AGE 37 WHITE MALE LABORER MURDER HANGING JUN 6 1890 JEFFERSON COUNTY.

King shot Fogarty, the manager of the dance hall in Elkhorn, on Thanksgiving. Apparently, Fogarty objected to King dancing with another man which resulted in the shooting.

18. ANTLEY NATIVE AMERICAN MALE MURDER HANGING DEC 19 1890 1 MISSOULA COUNTY

19. LALA, SEE NATIVE AMERICAN MALE MURDER HANGING DEC 19 1890 2 MISSOULA COUNTY

20. PIERRE, PAUL NAT. AMER. MALE ? MURDER HANGING DEC 19 1890 3 MISSOULA

21. PASCALE NATIVE AMERICAN MALE MURDER-ROBBERY HANGING DEC 19 1890 MISSOULA COUNTY

FOUR HUNG TOGETHER:

Pierre Paul, Lala See, Pascale, and Antley were executed on December 19, 1890 at the Missoula County Jail in Missoula, Montana. All four condemned men belonged to the Kootenai tribe. Pierre Paul and Lala See were convicted of killing two white men near Lala See's place on the Flathead Reservation. Pascale was convicted of killing a white man, reportedly for the man's horse. Antley, described as "young enough to be called a boy", was convicted of killing a white prospector. In the fall of 1887, Antley and five other boys were traveling to a ceremonial sun dance. After camping for the night, they reportedly discovered white men camped nearby. The group stealthily attacked the white prospectors and killed all three. One of the boys was later captured and lynched by angry miners in the area, but Antley and the rest of the young Indians were not apprehended until the summer of 1888. The young Indian men admitted guilt but they viewed their crimes as RETALIATION for whites killing Indians.

I, the author, have some thoughts on the plight of the Indians. The old saying, "The only good Indian is a dead Indian." was so much a part of western history. The atrocities were dealt out by both Indian and White. The white man's punishments were usually hanging; the Indian's punishment was killing the white man.

White Americans, particularly those who lived on the western frontier, often feared and resented the Native Americans they encountered. To them, American **Indians** seemed to be an unfamiliar alien people who occupied land that white settlers wanted.

From the birth of our country to today, we seized 1.5 billion acres of **native land**.

In 1887, Montana hadn't even become a state. Some thoughts from two Sioux Chiefs :

Chief Luther Standing Bear -Oglala Sioux stated the following:

"We did not think of the open plains, the beautiful rolling hills, and the winding streams with tangled growth as "wild." Only to the white man was nature a "wilderness," and only to him was the land "infested" with "wild" animals and "savage" people. To us, it was tame. Earth was bountiful, and we were surrounded with the blessings of the Great Mystery. Not until the hairy man from the East came and with brutal frenzy heaped injustices upon us and the families we loved was it "wild" for us. When the very animals of the forest began fleeing from his approach, then it was for us the "Wild West" began.

Sitting Bull's words from *Touch the Earth* by T. C. McLuhan:

"What treaty that the whites have kept has the red man broken? Not One. What treaty that the white maneuver made with us have they kept? Not One. When I was a boy, the Sioux owned the world; the sun rose and set on their land. They sent ten thousand men to battle. Where are the warriors today? Who slew them? Where are our lands? Who owns them? What white man can say I ever stole his land or a penny of his money? Yet, they say I am a thief. What white woman, however lonely, was ever captive or insulted by me? Yet, they say I am a bad Indian. What white man has ever seen me drunk? Who has ever come to me hungry and unfed? Who has seen me beat my wives or abuse my children? What law have I broken? Is it wrong for me to love my own? Is it wicked because my skin is red? Because I am Sioux; because I was born where my father lived; because I would die for my people and my country."

The Indian Removal Act was signed into law on May 28, 1830 by United States President Andrew Jackson. The law authorized the president to negotiate with southern Native American tribes for their removal to federal territory west of the Mississippi River in exchange for white settlement of their ancestral lands. Sitting Bull was born in 1831. He lived to see the Indians move west and then onto Reservations- a totally different life a penned up life in comparison to the freedom they did have prior to the white man's move throughout America.

22. BURNS, JOHN WHITE MALE TRANSIENT MURDER HANGING DEC 16 1892 MISSOULA COUNTY.

John Burns shot John Higgins. Apparently, Burns was a jewel thief and planned to kill his partner in crime, and accidentally shot Mr. Higgins.

23. ANDERSON, ROBERT AGE 26 WHITE MALE MURDER-ROBBERY HANGING JUL 13 1894 PARK COUNTY.

Unable to find any history on Robert Anderson.

24. OSNES, JOHN WHITE MALE MURDER-ROBBERY HANGING JUL 13 1894 CHOTEAU COUNTY

Unable to find out who John Osnes murdered and robbed.

25. CHRISTIE, CALVIN AGE 31 WHITE MALE PAINTER MURDER-ROBBERY HANGING DEC 21 1894 FLATHEAD COUNTY..

Calvin Christie, a.k.a. Charles Black, was convicted of the bludgeoning death of Mrs. Lena Cunningham, who resided near Columbia Falls in Flathead County. After an apparent rape, the victim's head was crushed, and she was left in a pool of her own blood. The hanging was the first held in Flathead County,

26. PUGH, CLAY AGE 24 WHITE MALE MURDER HANGING JULY 1, 1895 JEFFERSON COUNTY.

Pugh murdered C.W. West, a Conductor of the Butte, Anaconda, and Pacific Railroad. Pugh and some friends had gotten on the train illegally, and Mr. West stopped the train and removed them. Again, they were on the train and again Mr. West stopped the train and removed them. As soon as Pugh was put off the train, he fired 2 shots killing Conductor West.

27. CADOTTE, JOSEPH NAT. AMER. MALE TRAPPER MURDER HANGING DEC 27 1895 CHOTEAU COUNTY.

From the Northern Montana News December of 1895: The crime for which Cadotte was executed was the deliberate murder of Oliver Richards, a half breed companion. The crime was committed at the Penault Ranch some distance from Ft. Benton. After shooting his victim, Cadotte jumped on a horse and escaped, and the most active work on the part of the Sheriff failed to locate him. He was arrested by Indian Police on the Flathead Reservation and brought to Ft. Benton for trial. In 1892, Cadotte had shot a cowboy named Turnbull at Big Sandy. He was sent to Deer Lodge for one year. While a patient at the state hospital, he made a desperate attempt to murder an attache named Ubelman and nearly succeeded.

NOTE: Men's beliefs in the late 1800's; "with Cadotte's hanging, his death will have a salutary effect on the half breeds of this area, and will do much towards making them respecters of law and order."

In 1895, Sheriff Henry Jurgen would send out a public invitation, inviting the citizenry "to witness the execution of William Gay and William Biggerstaff" at the county jail.

28. BIGGERSTAFF, JOHN BLACK MALE MURDER HANGING APR 6 1896 LEWIS AND CLARK COUNTY.

Biggerstaff was a former slave from Lexington, Kentucky who had moved out West to Montana after gaining his freedom. In 1895, Biggerstaff was accused of murdering the African American prizefighter, Dick Johnson, in a quarrel over a white woman. Although Biggerstaff claimed the killing was done in self-defense, he was nonetheless found guilty and hanged.

29. GAY, WILLIAM AGE 52 WHITE MALE MINE OWNER MURDER HANGING JUN 8 1896 LEWIS AND CLARK COUNTY.

William ('Bill') Gay, was a frontiersman and businessman and a killer of two lawmen. Prior to that, he had killed a man named Forbes for being too enamored with Gay's wife. History.net has quite a write up on William Gay. From what I read it seems he was a man who, if he hadn't had bad luck, wouldn't have had any luck at all. He swore he was innocent right to the end.

30. SALMON, THOMAS WHITE MALE MINER MURDER HANGING JAN 27 1899 CARBON COUNTY.

Salmon was a union man and coal miner. A strike that he was involved in caused him to be fired. When he asked why and was still not rehired, he shot Mr. O'Connor, the supervisor of the mining company.

31. ALLEN, JOSEPH AGE 21 WHITE MALE LABORER MURDER-ROBBERY HANGING SEP 14 1899 LEWIS AND CLARK COUNTY.

Unable to find any history on Joseph Allen.

32. BROOKS, WILLIAM BLACK MALE HANDYMAN MURDER HANGING NOV 24 1899 YELLOWSTONE COUNTY.

William C. Brooks, a former soldier found guilty of murdering his wife in cold blood on Billings' South Side a year and six days earlier.

33. CALDER, WILLIAM AGE 27 WHITE MALE RANCH HAND MURDER-ROBBERY HANGING MAR 18 1900 FERGUS COUNTY

His execution was the first and only "legal" hanging in Fergus County, Montana. Calder was convicted of killing Farquar McRae and John Allen, sheep ranchers, near Lewistown, Montana.

34. HURST, JOSEPH WHITE MALE DEPUTY SHERIFF MURDER HANGING MAR 29 1900 DAWSON COUNTY.

On this date in 1900, Deputy Joseph Hurst hanged in Glendive, Montana for murdering Sheriff Cavanaugh. Hurst expressed his innocence to the end. His family, including his wife and two children, were allowed to visit him. Deputy Hurst is buried in Wadena, Minnesota.

35. PEPO, WILLIAM AGE 48 WHITE MALE LABORER MURDER-ROBBERY HANGING APR 6 1900 TETON COUNTY.

William Pepo murdered Julius Plath, a man he had traveled with. Circumstantial evidence was used.

36. LUCEY, DANIEL AGE 42 WHITE MALE MINER MURDER-ROBBERY HANGING SEP 14 1900 SILVER BOW COUNTY.

Executed for the murder of Patrick Reagan. They had been seen traveling together. Circumstantial Evidence was used.

37. FLEMING, JIM WHITE MALE EX CONVICT CONSP TO MURDER HANGING SEP 6 1901 POWELL COUNTY.

Fleming was hanged for the murder of Captain Oliver Dotson. Fleming was paid $15000 to shoot the elderly man by the man's son, Clinton Dotson.

38. DOTSON, CLINT WHITE MALE CONVICT CONSP TO MURDER HANGING APR 4 1902 POWELL COUNTY

Guilty of murder- for- hire in the killing of his father, Captain Oliver Dotson by Jim Fleming.

39. MARTIN, JAMES WHITE MALE MURDER-ROBBERY HANGING FEB 23 1904 SILVER BOW COUNTY.

Murdered Fireman Williams.

40. MOTT, LOUIS WHITE MALE LAUNDRY OWNER MURDER HANGING MAR 18 1904 MISSOULA COUNTY

Was executed for shooting his wife. He was hanged on what was called The Galloping Gallows.

41. METZGER, HERBERT WHITE MALE FARMER MURDER-ROBBERY HANGING MAY 5 1905 MEAGHER COUNTY.

Metzger was convicted of killing Homer Ward, Sheep Creek, Montana.

42. LU, SING ASIAN MALE MURDER HANGING APR 20 1906 GALLATIN COUNTY

A Bozeman Hanging: The Story of Lu Sing. At one time in the past, Bozeman had a significant Chinese population. Brought to the West by railroad or gold mining work, many Chinese people settled in Bozeman. Most Chinese businesses and homes were located in what was called 'China Alley,' the alley just north of Main Street between North Rouse and North Bozeman Avenues. There were several Chinese owned laundries, restaurants, and general stores located in this area.

On the morning of Tuesday, October 3rd in 1905, Tom Sing sat down for breakfast in the kitchen of the City Restaurant, a Chinese- owned place located on the corner of Main and Bozeman. Policeman Williams was making his rounds nearby and heard a scream from a Mrs. Maud Gilday. "They've cut Tom's head off, come quick!" Policeman Williams found Tom Sing on the floor with his head split open and his suit coat slashed to pieces. The policeman asked the nearby restaurant owner, who had committed this crime? The restaurant owner pushed forward Lu Sing, a Chinese man who had been employed by the City Restaurant for a short time as a handyman. "You take him," the restaurant owner said. Lu Sing offered no resistance and was immediately arrested and taken to jail.

The hanging took place at 1:05am on April 20th in 1906. Lu Sing's last words were, "I want to notify my cousin in Butte. I want to notify you people that I never kill anyone." Lu Sing is buried near the Poor Farm section in Sunset Hills Cemetery. The location of Lu Sing's grave is recorded in city records, but there is no marker remaining. Either the marker has been lost over time or more likely, no marker was erected.

Sources: Republican Courier, April 10, 1906, Three Forks Herald, February 19, 1981 Fergus County Argus, April 27, 1906 The River Press, November 15, 1905

Anne Garner, Who's Who in the Bozeman Cemetery (Bozeman: The Bozarts Press, 1987).

43. FULLER, MILES AGE 66 WHITE MALE MINER MURDER HANGING MAY 18 1906 SILVER BOW COUNTY.

In a feud over ore thefts from their placer mines, Fuller shot Henry J. Gallahan numerous times.

44. ROCK, GEORGE AGE 35 WHITE MALE CONVICT MURDER HANGING JUN 15 1908 POWELL COUNTY.

Rock and Hayes killed Deputy Warden John Robinson and severely wounded Warden Frank Conley in an escape attempt. Warden Conley was severely injured as he fought the criminals using his gun for a club. The criminals had knives and had attempted to escape.

45. HAYES, WILLIAM WHITE MALE CONVICT MURDER HANGING APR 7 1909 POWELL COUNTY.

Convicted of killing Deputy Warden Robinson.

46. LEBEAU, FREDERICK WHITE MALE MURDER HANGING APR 2 1909 FLATHEAD COUNTY.

Lebeau, who was hanged at Kallspell, was convicted of the murder of William F. Yoakum and Riley R. Yoakum near Fortine in Flathead county. Lebeau killed the Yoakums because they ordered him off their place and refused to sell him food.

47. COLLINS, JC BLACK MALE MURDER HANGING BY MONTANA MOB APRIL 4, 1913 SHERIDAN COUNTY.

Collins murdered Sheriff Thomas Courtiwy and shot Undersheriff Richard Burmeister 5 times; Burmeister died later from his wounds. They were attempting to arrest Collins for disturbing the peace. Burmeister was 33 years old and had been on the job for 4 months. The mob hung Collins up on a telephone pole then set fire to his clothing in an attempt to cremate him. They riddled his swaying body with bullets.

48. HALL, HENRY BLACK MALE HOBO MURDER-ROBBERY HANGING FEB 16 1917 MEAGHER COUNTY.

49. GIBSON, HARRISON BLACK MALE HOBO MURDER-ROBBERY HANGING FEB 16 1917 MEAGHER COUNTY.

50. FAHLEY, LESLIE BLACK MALE HOBO MURDER-ROBBERY HANGING FEB 16 1917 MEAGHER COUNTY.

Hall, Gibson, and Fahley were among 7 men (railroad workers) who attacked and robbed 3 men on another train. They shot their victims after they robbed them.

TRIPLE HANGING

51. POWELL, SHERMAN BLACK MALE PULLMAN PORTER MURDER HANGING JAN 14 1918 SILVER BOW COUNTY.

52. ONEILL, JOHN WHITE MALE MURDER-ROBBERY HANGING JAN 14 1918 SILVER BOW COUNTY.

53. FISHER, FRANK WHITE MALE MURDER-ROBBERY HANGING JAN 14 1918 SILVER BOW COUNTY.

TRIPLE HANGING takes place on Butte scaffold. John O'Neill, Frank Fisher and Sherman Powell hang for their crimes. Fisher & O'Neill protest their innocence. Powell had nothing to say and even smiled at the spectators in the court room.

54. CUELLAE, JOHN AGE 30 HISPANIC MALE LABORER MURDER HANGING APR 12 1918 YELLOWSTONE COUNTY.

For murder of Officer Nelson. He was the 2nd and the last man to be hanged in Yellowstone County.

55. LANE, ALFRED AGE 36 WHITE MALE FARMER MURDER HANGING SEP 3 1920 ROSEBUD COUNTY.

Alfred Lane was the first one of those hung on what was called The Galloping Gallows. It was moved throughout the state to wherever a hanging was to take place. Lane had murdered a local rancher, Harry Theade of Hathaway.

56. YICK, ALBERT AGE 29 WHITE MALE ESCAPED CONVICT MURDER HANGING AUG 26 1921 BEAVERHEAD COUNTY.

Yick was convicted of the murder of Sheriff Wyman.

57. VUCKOVICH, JOE AGE 34 WHITE MALE CRIMINAL MURDER HANGING FEB 17 1922 MISSOULA COUNTY.

5000 signatures pleaded for life in prison but Vuckovich was hanged. Even with a noose around his neck in a stockade behind the Missoula jail, Joe Vuckovich swore he hadn't murdered Mrs. Jerry Shea. "I am losing my life as innocent as any man that ever was hung," the 33-year-old Serbian maintained in broken but clear English on a February morning in 1922. Nora (Goff) Shea was shot dead on Missoula's Northside on Feb. 12, 1921. Vuckovich was there and then he wasn't, leading authorities on a manhunt that ended with his capture four days later 35 miles east of town. Tom Donovan, in his 2007 book, *Hanging Around the Big Sky*, said Vuckovich was the last man in Montana to be put to death on a jerk-type gallows. A 320-pound weight was dropped, pulling the 140-pound Vuckovich off the ground and breaking his neck. Two hundred invited guests watched.

58. REAGIN, JOSEPH AGE 22 WHITE MALE FARM HAND MURDER HANGING FEB 9 1923 TREASURE COUNTY.

For murdering Deputy Keeler. Bolton also involved. DOUBLE HANGING Bolton & Reagin.

59. GLENNA BOLTON AGE 29 WHITE FARMER MURDER HANGING FEB 9 1923 2 TREASURE COUNTY.

Undersheriff Irving Keeler was shot and killed by two men (Reagin & Bolton) he was arresting on a charge of petty theft.

Both men were convicted of murder and hanged on February 9, 1923. Undersheriff Keeler had served with the Treasure County Sheriff's Office for one year and was survived by his wife and two children.

60. HARRIS, WILLIAM WHITE MALE MURDER HANGING APR 20 1923 SILVER BOW COUNTY.

61. HARRIS, MONTE AGE 23 WHITE MALE MURDER HANGING APR 20 1923 SILVER BOW COUNTY These men who were not related were convicted of killing a hotel desk clerk.

DOUBLE HANGING

61. DANNER, SETH WHITE MALE MIGRANT FARM WKR MURDER-ROBBERY HANGING JUL 18 1924 GALLATIN COUNTY.

Danner had been accused of the 1920 murders of John and Florence Sprouse, but was only convicted of Florence's murder. His conviction rested largely on the testimony of his wife, Iva Danner, who testified that on Nov. 14, 1920, her husband "used an axe to crush Mrs. Sprouse's skull with two severe blows" and then strangled the pregnant woman with "a whang string," Burlingame wrote. Iva Danner made a deathbed confession that her husband should never have been hanged for Florence's murder, the 1995 newspaper reported. It was she who had killed Florence Sprouse. From The Bozeman Daily Chronicle.

62. WALSH, ROY AGE 22 WHITE MALE MECHANIC MURDER-ROBBERY HANGING FEB 15 1925 JEFFERSON COUNTY.

Roy Walsh was convicted of the cold- blooded shooting of store owner Albert Johnson of Whitehall.

63. VETTERE, TONY WHITE MALE MINER MURDER HANGING JAN 1 1926 SILVER BOW COUNTY.

Vettere had gone on a shooting spree in Butte killing three men and leaving 18 children fatherless.

64. SCHLAPS, FERDINAND AGE 19 WHITE MALE RANCH HAND MURDER-ROBBERY HANGING MAY 20 1927 ROOSEVELT COUNTY.

Schlapps murdering Mr. and Mrs. Anton Geisler and stealing their vehicle.

65. DAVISSON, ROLLIN AGE 44 WHITE MALE LABORER MURDER HANGING NOV 6 1929 PARK COUNTY.

Davisson walked in to the Livingston Police Station and shot Police Chief Holt and a Patrolman that was setting next to Holt.

66. HOFFMAN, GEORGE 45 WHITE MALE BARBER MURDER-ROBBERY HANGING AUG 29 1933 CHOTEAU County.

Murdered George Burrel by hitting him over the head with a pipe. His motive was robbery.

67. ZORN, HENRY AGE 26 WHITE MALE EX CONVICT MURDER-BURGLARY HANGING APR 24 1935 CUSTER COUNTY.

Zorn had spent time in the Pine Hills Reform School and Deer Lodge. He was robbing a safe in the Pine Hills Administration building when Lester Jones walked in. Lester was an Instructor and a son-in-law of the Superintendent. Lester did not think Zorn would shoot but he did; three shots killing Lester on the spot. Zorn was hung on a portable wooden gallows in the Miles City Jail.

68. GRINER, GEORGE AGE 38 BLACK MALE LABORER MURDER HANGING JAN 16 1935 CUSTER COUNTY.

George Griner was convicted of murdering his Negress Companion, Mrs. Mary Allsup. He also confessed to the murder of Police Sergeant James Fraser. Griner went to his death through the trap door of a scaffold in the Custer County Jail.

69. ROBIDEAU, FRANKLIN AGE 49 WHITE MALE RANCH HAND MURDER-ROBBERY HANGING JAN 15 1938 STILLWATER COUNTY.

He was hanged for the murder of husband and wife, Michael and Frieda Kunz of Columbus, Montana on November 26, 1937. He was the only man to be legally hanged in Stillwater County, Montana. On the fateful day he had gone to the Occidental Grain Elevator to get paid for 180 bushels of grain that he had delivered. Mike Kuntz, manager of the grain elevator, explained to Robideau that he could only be paid for two-thirds of the grain because one-third belonged to the man who owned the farm that Robideau worked. Robideau forced Kuntz to write him several checks and warned him against saying anything.

Fearful that Mr. Kunz and his wife would say something, he murdered them.

70.   SIMPSON, LEE AGE 52 WHITE MALE FARMER MURDER HANGING DEC 30 1939 GOLDEN VALLEY COUNTY.

Simpson had murdered Undersheriff Arthur "Buzz" Burford.

71.   COLEMAN, PHILLIP, JR. AGE 24 BLACK MALE RAILROAD WORKER MURDER-ROBBERY HANGING SEP 10 1943 MISSOULA COUNTY.

Coleman's crime was described at the beginning of this story.

There were so many hangings and also the hanging of Indians that were never recorded. Men, and I'm sure women, lost in the dust bin of our State's history. The following is a sad story:

A Native American Incident that ended when the Indians hung themselves in the Miles City Jail. :

Background: During the Northern Cheyenne Exodus in January 1879, Black Coyote, his wife Buffalo Calf Road Woman (she is famously known for saving her brother in the Battle of Rosebud, which was the reason why the Cheyennes called it, ("The battle where the girl saved her brother"), their two small children, his brother-in-law Whetstone, Hole in the

Breast, and other members of his family were part of Little Wolf's band of Northern Cheyenne who were traveling north to the Powder River Country. Black Coyote stole some horses with U.S. army brands, and one of the chief's named Black Crane told him to return the horses for the safety of the group. Black Coyote opposed this, and when Black Crane raised his whip, Black Coyote shot and killed him. Because of this, he and his family (totaling eight people) were banished from the tribe.

The incident:

On Saturday, April 5, 1879 in present-day Powder River or Custer County, Montana, near the crossing of Mizpah Creek by the Fort Keogh to Deadwood telegraph line, Sergeant Kennedy of the U.S. Signal Corps, and Private Leo Baader of Company E, 2nd U.S. Cavalry were repairing the line, when Black Coyote's party found and attacked them. The warriors killed Private Baader, severely wounded Sergeant Kennedy, and captured the two men's horses. The wounded Sergeant crawled into a bush, and drove off the warriors with his revolver, but not before Black Coyote took Baader's carbine and watch. Kennedy was later rescued after a great loss of blood by three civilians traveling from Deadwood, South Dakota, including a Mr. O'Neil, who helped him about 45 miles northwest to Fort Keogh. After learning details of the event on April 8, 1879, Colonel Nelson A. Miles, the commander of Fort Keogh, ordered out Sergeant Thaddeus B. Glover with a small detachment of ten soldiers of the 2nd U.S. Cavalry to locate and arrest the warriors responsible. A small detachment from Fort Ellis consisting of men from Company D, 2nd Cavalry under Captain Thomas J. Gregg also traveled in pursuit of the Lakota band. On April 10, 1879, Glover's men caught up with the Cheyenne's trail and deployed to advance. Two of the Cheyenne warriors signaled a white flag and willingly surrendered to Glover's detachment before the remaining warrior fired on the cavalrymen. The soldiers then forced the three warriors' surrender without taking any casualties and captured the five women and children. Black Coyote had with him articles of clothing and the watch taken from the body of Private Baader on April 5. The eight captured Cheyenne were then brought back to Fort Keogh. As the case was adjudged to be a civil one, the three warriors involved were housed in the Custer County jail at Miles City. During their imprisonment, Buffalo Calf Road Woman, the wife of Black Coyote, died of diphtheria in Miles City. When Black Coyote learned of this, he became crazy and did not eat nor sleep.

From May 27 to June 4, 1879, their case was heard in the first territorial court held in Montana Territory east of Bozeman. Present as a reporter for *The New York Times* was Thompson R. McElrath who on June 8, 1879 wrote a lengthy letter describing the trial. The verdict of June 4 was for the three warriors to be executed by hanging on July 7, 1879 but the next morning, June 5, the two hanged themselves in the jail at Miles City, Montana Territory. Later, the third Cheyenne also hanged himself in the jail.

The action of April 10, 1879, as recalled by Sergeant T. B. Glover:

"We were then in the Little Bighorn Mountains; I advanced but a short distance, when I saw two Indians standing on a rock silhouetted against the background of the sky, signaling with the white flag. I advanced and accepted the surrender. Turning, I heard the sound of furious firing in the rear. The two Indians had been joined by others and treacherously opened an attack while my men were quietly leaning on their arms. Not an Indian got away. We captured them all, and under a strong guard, I took them back to the post. They were tried and convicted of murder but cheated the executioner, for Indian-like, they all hanged themselves in the jail at Miles City.

United States Army
-Detachment at Mizpah Creek, April 5, 1879.
Sergeant Kennedy, U. S. Signal Corps, (severely wounded).
Private Leo Baader, Company E, 2nd U. S. Cavalry Regiment, (killed).
Detachment from Fort Ellis, April, 1879.

Soldiers of Company D, 2nd U.S. Cavalry Regiment, Captain Thomas J. Gregg (Co. D).
Detachment from Fort Keogh, April 7,-10, 1879.

11 Soldiers of Companies B and E, 2nd U. S. Cavalry Regiment, Sergeant Thaddeus Brown Glover (Co. B).

3 Indian Scouts.

Native Americans, Northern Cheyenne banished from Little Wolf's band.

3 Warriors, Black Coyote (committed suicide), Whetstone (committed suicide), and Hole in the Breast (committed suicide).

3 Women, Buffalo Calf Road Woman (died of Diphtheria in Miles City)

2 Children.

EPILOGUE

Law Enforcement has always been on the front lines protecting citizens from criminals. I was amazed at how many Sheriffs and their Deputies were murdered in the "old days."

Montana became a state in 1889, the same year my Grandmother was born in Indian Territory, OK/AR border. Montana's population was 142,924 in 1890. By 2019 Montana had 1.069 million. Montana ranked 19th in the nation for violent crimes in 2020.

It is sad to acknowledge the fact that as long as there are humans there will be violent crimes.

www.ingramcontent.com/pod-product-compliance
Lightning Source LLC
LaVergne TN
LVHW021742060526
838200LV00052B/3419